ABOUT THE AUTHOR

Jemma Hathaway was born on a Friday, because even then she couldn't wait for the weekend. Her poems have been featured on BBC Radio Bristol, BBC iPlayer and @bbc on Instagram. Jemma is a multiple slam-winner and was the 2020 Hammer & Tongue slam champion for Bristol. She is a *Button Poetry* Short Form contest winner, has appeared on Sky Arts *Life & Rhymes* and has supported Joelle Taylor, Jasmine Gardosi and Roger McGough. She has performed at some amazing venues, including: WOMAD festival, the Royal Albert Hall and her mum's kitchen. She self-published her first poetry pamphlet, *January* in 2021. *I've been looking everywhere for you* is her first full collection.
You can follow her on Instagram @jemmahathaway

I've been looking everywhere for you

Jemma Hathaway

VERVE
POETRY PRESS
BIRMINGHAM

PUBLISHED BY VERVE POETRY PRESS
https://vervepoetrypress.com
mail@vervepoetrypress.com

All rights reserved
© 2024 Jemma Hathaway

The right of Jemma Hathaway to be identified as author of this work has been asserted in accordance with section 77 of the Copyright, Designs and Patents Act 1988.

No part of this work may be reproduced, stored or transmitted in any form or by any means, graphic, electronic, recorded or mechanical, without the prior written permission of the publisher.

FIRST PUBLISHED MAY 2024

Printed and bound in the UK
by ImprintDigital, Exeter

ISBN: 978-1-913917-51-7

Cover Photograph by Simon Stone

For everyone I love

CONTENTS

If	11
If 2	13
How *love* came to be	14
My name was Gemma	15
A treatise on time	16
A smile will never knock a mirror off a wall	19
I read that 40% of women want a thigh gap and I think about the Mona Lisa	21
To the young ones who feel alone and can't come out right now	22
To the hunters of light, the lovers of life and the makers of music	26
Dear Scarlett	30
Girls to all other girls	31
Squiggles	32
When you're looking for a sign	34
How *grief* came to be	35
When I say friendship	36
Goodbye is dropped from the dictionary	37
All the answers are in an eighties movie	38
Anxiety: a gentle reminder	42
Anxiety: a gentle reminder - *addendum*	43
Imposter syndrome	44
Pep talk for self talk	45

The poem that climbed a mountain to tell you this	46
Words for my Welsh uncle's funeral flowers	48
Words for my mum's 'just because' flowers	49
The water cycle	50
Some things I know	51
The day I discovered miracles	54
J	55
Soft words for hard times	56
You matter	57
The love that dare not speak its name has never stopped talking	60
My dad was a submariner for thirty years and then he got a Goldwing	63
Compliments to the chef	65
To the United States Supreme Court and other such similar decision-makers	66
Being a black girl in the nineties in a town where there are hardly any black girls	69
How *forever* came to be	70
A note on the usage of the word 'woman' for those who need it	71
Laws of war	73
On the bad days, this is for you	75
To thirteen-year-old me	78
To thirteen-year-old me - *a further note*	81
Four billion beautiful things	82
To regret	86
My melanin	87

How *carefree* came to be	90
How to stop your spiralling head with your soaring heart	91
How *healing* came to be	95
Home	96
To-do list for a life	98
The end	102

Acknowledgements

I've been looking everywhere for you

The most misspelled word
in the English language is

separate -

we can't make sense
of being apart.

If

If some days self-belief is a high-school cafeteria
and nobody will let you sit with them,

if all your wishing wells
are into their overdrafts,

if you are an awkward triangle
trying to find your way inside the circle -
everyone else seems so well-rounded,

if they found the key to a secret
and you are still searching for a locksmith,

if you feel like an apology note
trying to be an acceptance speech,

if the world is tribal
and somehow you were born outside
the city limits of the Earth,

if you are a forgetful piano
often losing your keys,

if your infrastructure
feels like bad town planning,

if you battle anxiety so often
you're certain worrier and warrior
are the same word,

if serotonin plays Hide and Seek
and you are always the one
counting to ten,

if you misspell
separate,

I've been looking everywhere for you.
I'm so glad we found each other.

If 2

If I could make a voodoo doll of myself
I would whisper in its ear every morning,
you are amazing, don't let you
tell you any different.

How *love* came to be

Once upon a time a cartographer met a cardiologist. Together they learned how to map hearts.

My name was Gemma

but a maternity nurse
wrote Jemma on my chart
and set the tone for a lifetime -
always intending to be one thing
turning out to be another.

So many things were something else once -
the first oranges were green,
every wrinkle began its journey as a good joke,
every river was a raincloud,
every window started out as sand.

When you walk barefoot on the beach
you step on an origin story,
you tread on tomorrow's glass,
everything changes and that's okay -
just while you can
enjoy the feel of eternity
between your toes.

A treatise on time

On 20th August 1949
so many starlings roosted
on the minute hand of Big Ben
they stopped time.

If a light-year is distance
then a heavy-foot can be time -
how it stamps on us all.

In a lifetime a heart has
about three billion beats,
because time is money -
we are all the best kind of billionaires.

Collect old calendars
and drop them down the slender necks
of wishing wells as legal tender(ness,)
get those good years back

back, back to the day you were a twinkle
in your parents' eyes
or to the twinkle that came before them
or back to when twinkles
were still theories
nobody had proven yet and say,
you won't believe it, but the future is bright
and we are wasting it scrolling in the dark.

When I was ten
I played Fizzy
in *Bugsy Malone*,
stood onstage alone
and sang a solo of 'Tomorrow' -
sometimes I wonder
what happened
to the kid carrying future
in her throat.

Now I try to tell myself
there are only so many todays left,
don't waste them looking back at the yesterdays
you spent singing of tomorrows.

If you look out the window
of your life
whatever the sky looks like
it's later than you think.

You're not going to last forever.
You are not a playlist,
you're a mixtape -
you only have so many minutes
to fit everything in.

We often say things too late,
think there will be more time,
believe the clock will always be there
winding us onward
anxious to get us to that next second -
we forget the person is the clock.

Someday a thousand starlings
will roost on the minute hand of your heart
and you will fail the test of time.
When that instant arrives, I hope
you remember all the beautiful moments
you stopped to feed the birds,
because I promise
time flies.

A smile will never knock a mirror off a wall

Some mornings
happiness is a houseplant
you forget to water,

joy is a fuse switch that keeps tripping
the light, fantastic
is a word someone made up once.

On these mornings
you are a cutlery drawer
with too many knives and not enough spoons,

you feel so fragile
your teardrops
need parachutes,

decide if your delight
was written in the stars
even the universe makes spelling mistakes.

On these mornings
you do not chew kale
or do downward dog,

or high five the fucking mirror
like that podcast
told you to try last week,

you do not meditate
or count backwards for some reason
or swallow anything fermented.

On these mornings
you eat biscuits for breakfast,
dance round the kitchen

like it's the nineties
and your knees
still love themselves,

wonder how your girlfriend
got so great,
how your cats never have a down day -

this doesn't fix everything,
this doesn't change anything,
but it makes you smile.

On the mornings
your room is a raincloud
that smile is the best anorak
hanging in your wardrobe.

I read that 40% of women want a thigh gap and I think about the Mona Lisa

In 1911 when the Mona Lisa was stolen,
huge crowds gathered to see
the space where it had been.

I doubt a single one of those people
believed the empty space
was more perfect than the painting.

To the young ones who feel alone and can't come out right now

There are bad days
when you don't know
if you're more cliff or volcano
if you'll erupt or erode -

either way you're losing pieces of yourself.
But there will be a day soon
when you become the moon
and you'll make the tide turn.

You are not alone,
there's a whole world waiting to meet you here.
I promise time will not always seem so severe
you make an enemy of the clock,

long for tick to leave tock
to pursue a solo career,
soon the hands on your watch
will wave at you as they fly by.

And you'll wonder why
you ever thought
time was too slow
when your life will flow

like prosecco
at bottomless brunch.
Maybe right now you sit alone at lunch
sure you are a side dish

but you are the banquet.
Tomorrow can taste you
and asks for seconds, reckons
diners will dress up

just to sit down at your table
and thank their lucky stars
they even got an invitation,
you are not a lucky star

but the whole damn constellation.
In time the thirteenth sign
of the zodiac
will be your profile picture.

Or maybe you spend breaks
in a bathroom cubicle
and your best mate
is a Samsung S24

but a night will come
when all your besties
cram into a toilet stall together
you'll take a photo on your S29

look at it next morning sat on somebody's
sofa and love everything
about your life
except your hangover.

If now is a packed commuter train
you want to depart
I promise the day will arrive
when that someone eyes

you from across an otherwise
empty carriage
and you will never want
to reach your station.

It's all so close
your shadow just got jealous
and I swear to you
you're not a boomerang

though you're hell of a catch
you'll never have to come back
to these moments,
the future has a lasso

swinging right at you.
Soon so many people will spend
their dreams, hoping to look into your eyes

wishing wells will have to hang
no vacancy signs.
Remember, anything can be a song, if
you carry enough music on your lips -

someday so many of us are gonna stream
your smile on Spotify
Beyoncé will dedicate her next album
to the corners of your mouth.

When these moments are monochrome
just know, every rainbow
is your future self
leaving you love notes -

skywriting pride across time
to say, look how much colour
is coming for you.

I know it seems today
all the love is another language
and you have the wrong tongue,
but tomorrow you'll find the ones
who become Google Translate.

Hang in there, just you wait. One day
you won't have enough words to say
how glad you are to be gay.

To the hunters of light, the lovers of life and the makers of music*

After Buddy Wakefield

In September 1977, NASA sent the spacecraft Voyager 1 out into the
    universe.
At this very moment, it is the farthest manmade object from the
    poem in your hands.
Its cargo is a needle and a disc, bearing the inscription *to the makers*
    of music,
which if encountered by an advanced civilisation someday, will play
a selection of the sounds of Earth.
They called it the Golden Record.

What Chris Stapleton's *Traveller*
and the spacecraft Voyager
most have in common is that they are both a journey
best enjoyed on vinyl.

Chris Stapleton first sang 'Tennessee Whiskey'
on the spur of the moment during a soundcheck.
And the first time I started to think this was a big thing between us,
we were looking for light in the rain.

Big things happen in small moments.

In the guitar tune-up, lights on,
hoods-up, hearts out moments
when hopes and dreams get goosebumps
and souls start to wave at one another.

Since light itself is a wave
that first night we walked
around the Light Festival
just maybe, the world was waving back.

It was all giggle and drizzle and dazzle
and downpour, some of our best times so far
we've laughed through the rain.

Soaked to the skin, like up in
the hills under the sleeping-bag of the stars
when slugs and spiders on our tent felt like living
confetti, I never want nature to stop
throwing herself at us. Let's pray we'll always be kicking up dust together.

And a thousand years from now
when we're dust too, I bet we'll be that good dust you see dancing
in sunbeams shooting through skylights in happy kitchens,
give me a kitchen disco dust forever with you.

Let's swear to see it all someday
say soon, say one minute from now
paint a picture of tomorrow
and climb in that campervan before the paint dries.

There's no better soundtrack to us, than *Traveller*
let's pen love letters to the vanishing point
with the ink in our walking boots.
Dear Horizon, we're coming for you
there's no going back now

only forwards with light
feet. When self-belief
felt like brick, you hit
like a ton of feathers
and all the sadness started
to remember how to fly
away, and everything got so light, we might
still have been walking wet that night
the city turned on its torches, lit the way just for us
and we knew this thing was big –
the way chemistry is big, and electricity is big
and little details are biggest of all.

Every festival before you was a soundcheck.
Every song before us sounded like a CD
but now it's that good vinyl, that sounds sweeter
because we bought it together
that old analogue love -
they don't make them like this anymore.

All this time, we were never looking for perfect
we were looking for silly
and damn, didn't we find it.
If we promise each other anything, let it be
that we swear to stay weird as hell with one another,
to keep talking in the voices nobody else knows,
never stop our hands being magnets
and remember this right here is magic
is what they're all out there with metal detectors, looking for
just this, this happy, silly, gorgeous, ordinary, massive, shining,
    little life.

As long as the sun's up
or the rain's slamming down
we got good boots on our feet,
slow hands on our watches,
there's no need to worry
we've got everything we ever need,
it's hard to explain the little things
when *us* is the biggest word there is.

Just know, somewhere interstellar out there
on the edge of impossible
is a rocket-ship with a record
and some distant day when we're that dancing dust,
someone will dig up that time capsule from the depths of infinity,
touch that needle to the gold,
hear all the sounds of life as we know it

and it will be almost as special
as the nights the two of us sit together
with a tumbler and a turntable
and listen to 'Tennessee Whiskey.'

* *A commissioned poem for my friends, who fell in love like they were falling to Earth*

Dear Scarlett
or
Finding out you're going to be an auntie for the first time
or
If you want to know about love

Your mum didn't know quite what to do
so I held the ClearBlue
between her legs.

We may not always do our best work in exam conditions.

You are still the best answer on a test
I've ever seen.

Girls to all other girls

Text me when you get home.

Text me when you get
everything you ever wanted.

Either way
I always want to know you made it.

Squiggles

When she was five, my niece, Taylor
looked at my mother's face
and called the few lines she saw there,
squiggles.

I love that she made art
of every moment laughter
found itself a kite
caught in the branches
of my mother's skin

and realised it was better
to stick around
than fly away
a forgotten thing.

May every good giggle
grab hold of my face and refuse to let go.
If crow's feet mean I laughed a lot,
hell, I pray my eyes are an aviary
sketched with five-thousand feathers.

Comic books got their name
by starting life in newspapers
as the funny pages

and isn't that all we hope for,
that the funny pages of our lives
are written all over our faces.

Art was once an Olympic event -
may my life be so goddamn hilarious
in the end, fate looks at my face
sees a gallery and gives me the gold.

When you're looking for a sign

Since signs saying
beware of pickpockets
attract pickpockets,

I hope you erect signs on every street
of yourself, that say,
beware of joy.

How *grief* came to be

One day the cardiologist's heart retired.
The cartographer lost their way.

When I say friendship
After Meredith Martinez

Last winter my best friend died in his bed. Family came to check on him and found him cold. They broke the news to me down the phone and cried. Now it is autumn and I still have swimmer's ear. I don't think I will ever hear out of it again. It's the cold I find hard to believe. He had hyperhidrosis. Was always hot. Always wet with sweat. Last summer on the way to Pride, he bought a pack of three cheap chequered tea-towels. Wore them round his neck to soak himself up, like a prize-fighter ready for the final round. The last time I saw him, he walked to my parents' house in zero-degree weather, wearing Bermuda shorts. My mum gasped at his goose-pimples but every single one was the sound of his skin exhaling. Happiest when his body was frostier than his hair in the noughties. Parts of him were still warm. I wonder which parts, precisely. Which bits of his body clung like wet t-shirt. If these parts were the ones that wanted to stay. If one of them was mine. Back in the spring of ourselves, we'd pool every last penny to buy heart rhythms wrapped in squares of old lottery tickets. We rolled each other's cigarettes, licked each other's Rizlas and smoked each other's spit. Back then, I got so drunk, I pissed in his bed. He woke, rolled his eyes, we flipped the mattress and went back to sleep in each other's arms.
When I say friendship, that is what I mean.

Goodbye is dropped from the dictionary

I want to live in a world
where balloons mate with boomerangs.

It's easier to let go
if we know,

the things we love
will find a way back.

All the answers are in an eighties movie

You've lost count
of how many summers

you've been to Kellermans
to learn nothing

can soar in a corner
to know you can look

(Some Kind of)
Wonderful out there

you are Marty McFly clinging
to the back of life's

flatbed truck, sure your heart
was built to be a hoverboard

with the power of love
to stay up on its own

to not go that way
never go that way

if you keep going
that way

you'll go straight
to that castle

no matter how many times
you hear Gordy's stories

Chris is still going
to die in the end

you can't save him
but every time he tells

the better tale
about the milk money

and the dress with the dots on it
he still keeps right on saving you

when the lights go out
you just might be

the sixteen candles
somebody reaches for

you swear to One-Eyed Willy
you will never get in Troy's bucket

you're so grateful Ducky
taught you to try

a little tenderness
to realise queerness

is your best friend
before he ever knew

he was
queer himself

when the wolf
is at the door

stop letting it in
and the ball goes in the basket

if you fight enough skeletons
paint enough fences

you always get
the girl

and you can beat the bad guys
with one foot off the floor

some people refuse to listen
to your music

and you might step on the tracks
and scream at trains

but damnit
you dance your ass off anyway

then one day, it's all Ridgemont High
and the times are too fast

your Ride or Die
is a white horse

who sinks
in the sadness

and just maybe the story
does end

it's not how you fly
that makes you

a maverick
it's having a wingman, anytime

when they fly too far
you hope

they will find a way
to phone home

until then, you keep trying
to bust all your ghosts

with good friends
and a fuck-ton of marshmallow.

Anxiety: a gentle reminder

Don't speak your mind
speak your lungs instead.

Learn the language
of your own breath.

Exhale until nothing makes sense
but tectonic shifts in your chest.

So, when anxiety
loads bullets into the chambers

of your heart again
you only need

a stethoscope
at the gunfight.

Anxiety: a gentle reminder
- *addendum*

To never again use the chambers of my heart
as a metaphor for the chambers in a sidearm,

to always say, *ceasefire now*,
no matter whose gun threw the first punch.

Imposter syndrome

You try to see yourself
the way the world saw Titanic,

when iceberg was still idea.
But in the mirror

you see Carpathia,
searching for survival,

deck scattered with castaways
in other people's coats,

carrying the ocean
in their pockets.

Please try to tell yourself,
at least you turned up and stayed afloat.

Pep talk for self talk

You are a gasp
in the mouth of the universe
mistaking yourself for a sigh.

Click *hell no* when imposter syndrome
requests read receipts.

Remember your heart
has transferable skills

but it's not a baseball,
stop taking swings
at yourself

be the pitcher
go out there and throw

caution to the wind,
make the universe catch
it's breath.

I promise you'll be caught
by surprise.

The poem that climbed a mountain to tell you this

In September 2022, a friend climbed Kilimanjaro. She took these words with her, sealed in an envelope to be opened only in the event of a tough moment on the mountain.

I am certain of you

keep firing hope
out of the cannon in your chest

remember sweat
is saltwater

every time you break
into one, you make

an ocean
of yourself

there are ten thousand uncharted mountains
under the sea, so maybe

right now
you are one of them

conquer you
and everything else is just staircase

I swear if you lift the loose floorboards
of your feet

soon enough you'll find summit
hidden beneath

even if today, you don't feel strong enough to lift
the muscles in your face

mountains are the prime place
to find the light

so, fix solar panels to the roof
of your mouth

I promise the next sunrise
will pull your smile right up with it.

Words for my Welsh uncle's funeral flowers

Dylan Thomas wrote
do not go gentle into that good night,

but he never met you
so he never knew

how powerful gentle
could be

and since *Gareth* means *gentle* in Welsh
I hope you go Gareth into that good night.

Words for my mum's 'just because' flowers

Faith is the belief in things larger than ourselves.
I always have faith in your strength -
it's the biggest thing I know.

The water cycle
for Chris

On the days your dark clouds
are so close you have to duck

I hope you can
remember precipitation

it is thought raindrops
are shaped like tears

but they are spheres
little planets -

so, when worlds
are falling around you

tomorrow they might just
become puddles

if you feel weather
beaten

I hope you can remember
your skin is waterproof

you're a beautiful umbrella
not every day will turn you inside out.

Some things I know

I know this world makes you
feel small, that life seems
an expensive hobby
you are struggling to turn into a career.

There is no such tragedy
as the words, *cost of living crisis*.
I know this life is not a utility bill,

this heart is not a smart meter.
I also know if power is money

we are all light croupiers
dealing out lumens like playing cards
like fifty-two aces in the whole
of your heart.

I look at this life
and know the moon landing happened.

Physics explains how the universe behaves,
I know, there is nothing more
physics than poem. Science says
today the earth's axial tilt is 23.43632°
and it continues to turn
but I know sometimes the earth stops...
and stares when you walk by.

I know daylight savings time is a lie,
a prank so the sun can stay up late
and doodle your name in its diary.
It's a trick of the light
money can't buy.

I know this life
is all those hand in the air moments
when the beat breaks like a heart.
You want to get down on your knees
and sweep up every last piece of it,

pluck the acoustic heartstrings
on the fretboard of your ribs
in the skiffle band of your midsection,
I know you deserve better
than busking every moment
for the right to keep playing.

I know I will never go hunting -
all the things I want are already looking for *me*.
But I do believe in shooting
stars. I know the only good firearm
is a hot glue gun
in the hand of a *Drag Race* queen
who didn't learn to sew
before she went on the show.

I know the only thing rising faster than bills
is hopelessness.

I know the most beautiful thing I heard last year
was Marilyn Monroe
once wrote *hope hope hope*
on the back of one of her wedding photos,
hope as a treble
clef, musical notation
for butterflies in the orchestra pit
of our stomachs.

I quaver at the shifting beats of ourselves
and wonder if things will work out.

I know hope is a back-up generator.

I *hope hope hope* a stranger spills
a smile all over your new top.

I know I'm glad you sat here
and laid your eyes
on me, like you were laying down
in the grass.

I know it's hard to cultivate a garden heart
if your flowerbed feels emptier than your bank account
and you don't have two peonies to rub together.

But everything tough
helps you grow, so I know
how tall we are on the inside.

The day I discovered miracles

'There are only two ways to live your life. One is as though nothing is a miracle. The other is as though everything is.'
– Albert Einstein

The first time I saw Pink in concert was 2006 at Wembley Arena. The first words she sang were *Ice-cream, ice-cream, we all want ice-cream* and the place exploded like a diagram of what does joy look like. My girlfriend and I stood beside a blissful, drunk, middle-aged woman who told us she'd lost her dad somewhere in the crowd, that they went everywhere together. And I thought what a cool guy, rocking concerts in the standing section at his age. We stayed side-by-side for the whole show and danced together, the way you do when you meet someone you will never see again, but for a minute there, that stranger is a sonnet because your soul's rhyme for a short time. At the end she asked us to stay and help find her father. *He's very small*, she said. So, we waited until we were almost the only ones left in the standing section of the entire arena. Only then did she laugh, look down and begin to search the floor. She explained that she wore her father round her neck nowadays, that he existed only as ashes. So, we explored the world at our feet like kids searching for fairies, examining every inch of the floor for magic. And I swear this is true - I found her father. Intact. Whole as a body. In a glass orb, no bigger than a marble, or a cherry or a universe. There is a standing capacity of six thousand at Wembley Arena. And somehow, he didn't break. I handed him to his daughter. She thanked me and smiled like this happened every day. And we said goodbye forever. I like to think just maybe her dad was always playing these pranks. Just maybe they don't truly leave us, we only wear them differently. Just maybe they went out for ice-cream. The name of that tour? *I'm not Dead.*

J

Some of us called you *Jay*
you perfect capital letter -

all my favourite stories start with you
and end there too. Boy, if we went to prison

I swear we would
finish each other's sentences.

Joke and *jewel* come from the same Latin word
and both begin with you

because laughter
is like having diamonds in your mouth

and diamonds are a girl's best friend.
Thanks for being my favourite piece of jewellery.

Soft words for hard times

In London there are traffic bollards
that began life
as battle cannons

and east-end estates
ringed with protective fences
that were once Second World War stretchers.

I promise it is possible
to make a safe space
out of past pain.

I promise you will too.

You matter

the universe is thinking about you
tastes your name under its tongue

slams shots of your spirit
considers a big bang

behind your back
just to turn your head

you do not
think yourself worthy

of attention
the universe knows better

sorts your thoughts
into a playlist

and listens every time
you sing yourself songs

about all the things you did wrong
yesterday

when two pieces of metal meet in space
they become one

remain that way forever
have no way of knowing

they are not the same
it's called cold welding

the universe tries
to do this with you

knows to show not tell
so, speaks

in body language
because it is universal

nudges doorframes into your shoulder
skirting boards against your toes

lifts kerbs to trip you up
sends teacups

slipping from your fingers
finds all the way

to throw
its voice and show

the green cross code
is not only for the road

Stop. Look. Listen.

remember how precious you are
how delicate

these are the push notifications
of the universe

do not turn them off
galaxies planets nebulas

all that matter
needs you to pay attention

and believe
you matter.

The love that dare not speak its name has never stopped talking
After Peter Ackroyd

The love that dare not speak its name
sings instead,
becomes a choir.

When the world says
Don't raise your voice with me
we raise the roof,
rip spires off churches,
nightingales from our throats,
our songbirds peck
at the hymn book of history.

Since love means
never having to say you're sorry,
we are unapologetic for our karaoke.

How we sing the body electric
like pylons, our voices pile on
one another, we orgy of sound
we pillow talkers,
how you hear us through the walls
of time.

We jukebox at The Stonewall,
sound travels faster than bricks
so what is the first thing we know of riot
but its song, what is a pride march

but a queer stampede
we beautiful beasts stomping,
if they say we strike fear
I swear we only strike lightning,
how we thunder our hooves.

The love that dare not speak its name
sings instead,
becomes an instrument,
conducts itself a symphony
at the other end of the ballroom,

shoulders dressed
with confetti treble clefs,
we have never been bereft
of ways to find high notes in low moments,
soprano of survive
in the baritone of battleground,

how we play on,
like the string quartet that kept strumming
as Titanic slipped under the duvet of the sea,
if you hold time to your ear
you can still hear them plucking each other,

we crescendos,
we gorgeous singing kettles in god's kitchen,
how we turn each other on,

we seven-stringed guitars, we three-holed flutes
playing nine-bob notes,
we have always found ways to hold a tune
with voices tied behind our backs.

The love that dare not speak its name
stands onstage at the census
and performs its first recital,

1.5 million of us
singing our fucking hearts out,
singing our hearts in,

all opening our mouths at the same time,

the love that dare not speak its name
says, *I dare, I do dare*, there
is all this god given dare in my mouth
I will drop my jaw
and how you will lose your breath,

now every time we speak
that hammer in your ear
builds a goddamn house,
we erect so many neighbourhoods
our tongues are scaffolding planks

and this whole time in all this noise
in this cacophony, this opera,
the melody was so simple -

we just want to love each other

and that is all we were ever trying to say.
We were here the whole time

if you would just listen
you can hear us and

what a sound we are.

My dad was a submariner for thirty years and then he got a Goldwing *or* When a fish becomes a bird

When your years have been all at sea
and it is time for a gear change,

gold wings are the way the universe says -
the concierge of good times

has made you a central reservation
every road is expecting you.

Grab hope by the handlebars
and sit happiness in the passenger seat

that way it is always with you
holding on to your butterfly places.

Today may the motorway
be as open as your heart

and your heart as open
as New York's eyes,

ignore every hard shoulder
that doesn't make it all feel easy

and decide jams
only exist in jars.

A ladybird's wings
are four times the size of its body,

just as your joy is four times
the size of the engine - this is how it flies,

remember gold never rusts,
so, your wings will last forever.

Take your camshaft heart
and challenge the speedometer

to a race against amazement
where the finish line is the horizon

and somehow you will
all win,

on this Earth the tallest waterfall is under the sea
and the longest river is in the sky

this is all the proof you need
that sometimes beauty hides

under all those layers
of leather, your soul is a smile,

let it fuel every mile
the way Goldwings soar

and every roar
is the engine asking the highway to dance,

telling the world this is all just zen
and the heart of motorcycle maintenance.

Compliments to the chef

You try to be the sunflower
but often you're the oil,

thinking only of stoves
and spilling yourself into pans,

these are the times you're glad
she does all the cooking

knows her way so well
around this kitchen

can pick up your pot
make you solar-powered again,

how she moves you
into that sweet spot

of light
on the windowsill.

To the United States Supreme Court and other such similar decision-makers
After Roe v. Wade

I do not live in America
but I do live inside a body,

have done all my life
I was born and bred here,

this body
is my America -

it has the right to bear arms
around its shoulders,

but will never hold a gun in its hands
and call it defence.

In the Midwest of this body,
in the heartlands,

it will shout *freedom*
from every rooftop,

until your ears are as open
as the borders of this body,

should somebody seek refuge here,
because this body would not exist without immigration

and what are borders anyway, but scars
scratched into the Earth from old wars once,

if you read the map of this body
you will find thirty-nine scars that say,

some battles happened here
but it is still free,

refuses to make a statute
of liberty,

when it is older,
this face will have more lines

but will not ask you to prove citizenship
simply to look into its eyes.

Down in the Great Plains of this abdomen,
if I never choose to plant a tree here, some withered

old Republicans
will not make an orchard of it.

This uterus is indigenous,
this body is not Rushmore,

you cannot carve men's faces
into these mountains

and call it your landmark,
but if you still believe yourself Rock

I say to you,
keep my womb's name out your fucking mouth,

we have nothing
to say to one another -

except, if this body
was a body of water

you tried to traverse,
no matter how much you argued the merits

of row versus wade,
then I would tell you, *don't dare try to cross me.*

Being a Black girl in the 90s in a town where there are hardly any Black girls

In PE you are first to be picked,
at parties the last to be kissed.

Boys point at you and dare
each other to go there -

the same boys who, years later
friend request you on Facebook,

say you look like Halle Berry,
send you private messages

about how cool
your hair looks

now, but you remember the looks
they gave each other

when you were drinking down the park
everything started to spin

and the bottle
pointed at you.

Now they look like... that
and you have this skin,

revenge is a dish best served
with extra melanin.

How *forever* came to be

There was once a leaf
that refused to fall
and instead began a revolt
against the natural way of things

and learned that nature
was not a YouTube tutorial
and the natural way of things
was however the things of nature decided to be
and so the leaf spoke to its tree

and the tree stood its ground
told the world it would not be cut down
and turned into a bible
instead would prove divine
by all the engagement
rings on its insides

and so the many leaves
promised themselves to the tree
won tug of war with the wind
and never once wondered
what went on in the gutters in winter.

A note on the usage of the word 'woman' for those who need it

After Sarah Everard

Wrap your lips around the word.
Hold it on your tongue

until it feels uncomfortable there
and you understand

the word is not yours
to lick like an envelope

and put your stamp on.
Notice in the dark spaces

between the lines
how it can sound like *woah, man.*

Really listen to that.
Observe how part of it sounds like womb

because it carried every one of you
and *omen*, because it is a phenomenon –

every time you write the word *woman*
your pen can't believe it got so lucky.

Notice how *woman*
is another way to say *Queen*

because sometimes heavy
is the head that wears the crown

and lately it seems
there are not enough empty spaces

to lay the weight down.
But as time marches on,

we keep marching too
and watch us show you
what one word can do.

Laws of war

After Bobbi-Anne McLeod

To be a girl now
is to be a shield

in an armoury
in the backroom of a battlefield

with blueprints on becoming
a burial ground.

I'm British
I know invasion when I see it

when somehow a body becomes
a border to breach.

I'm grateful
for laws of war

but isn't it typical of humans
to agree wording

on the fairest ways
to destroy one another,

only this week
I began to wonder

when we will extend the Geneva Convention
beyond countries,

to the bodies of girls waiting
at bus-stops

and the minds of men
with no intention of boarding a bus.

On the bad days, this is for you

It's not easy.
There are times
when you don't want to look the day in the eye,
when the world only throws stones
and you are a glass house.

To stay gentle
in spite of all this,
is to be a gorgeous balloon
in a world of nail-bombs
and never fear the flight.
Lately you are finding it harder
to leave the ground.

Your heart is not always the place
you keep your love,
sometimes you leave it on the tip of your tongue,
for the moments you can't find the words
and all you have to offer is an apology.

Please don't say sorry for yourself -
someone made you feel small once
and you thought sorry was the fertiliser
that would get you growing again,
but nothing guilty ever grows.

And my god, don't you know
how perfect you are?
If you squint, really look for it,
I promise the horizon is holding out its hand
to pass you a party invitation -
I hope you accept.

Please start to say yes to yourself -
your mouth is a trapeze
and we hang on your every word,

your laughter is a doorbell -
every time it rings
someone's heart swings
open, so while you can,
let them in without checking first.

Because I promise, if you have a person
and they are still here -
you are the luckiest person alive.

Trust your vast noble heart
to the first noble gas,
there is so much lift, up
for grabs
in this life of yours.

I hope you can wake tomorrow
and remember what it was like
to learn to whistle,
for so long you didn't understand
why you couldn't do it
then one day, just like that,
it happened! You couldn't believe
how easy it was -
maybe learning joy is just like that.

On the unbelieving days,
I hope you can give a little whistle -
whistle so loud they stop a football match
on the other side of the Earth

and everyone starts clapping,
like they believe in fairies -
except they believe in something better,
they believe in you
and maybe you can too.

So, on delicate days
when you think yourself a glass house
and the world throws stones at you,
I know you can try, try real hard -
to be hopscotch.

To thirteen-year-old me

Everybody is busy
talking about boys

and you are hiding in the back row
of library books, breaking

school sprint records
trying to run away from yourself.

You think you'll never grow
out of all this, remember the universe was born

out of a pinprick that wanted more for itself.
When you feel high

as a molehill, that's still
evidence you turn the earth. I know you bury

teardrops in the pillow, but under
a microscope tears look like snowflakes

and the collective noun for snowflakes
is an avalanche -

every time you cry
you become a mountain,

all your fault lines
disrupt the skyline later

keep writing your lines
secret beat poet,

keep scribbling and reaching for the high
notes. There are flowers growing

out of guitars in your fingertips -
even when your internal organs

are only cheap keyboards the sheet music refuses
to sit still for, there's a bass here collecting dust

like Neighbours stickers you'd have swapped everything for once
so, keep pulling the strings, kid.

We're still unsure, we're still uncertain
little Libra-life-livers

hell, if you ask my favourite colour
I'll say rainbow,

ask our favourite mistake, I'll say every one
of them, they all dropped me off right here,

you don't know it yet, but I'm freaking
proud of you for trying to live

like the sky on six cylinders after it slung
all the clouds out the window, to say

I'm gonna be the next big thing
to keep going no matter how blue it becomes.

You're always banging
the headrests

from the backseat
of slow-moving classrooms, asking

*are we there yet
are we there yet?*

I want you to know
you're the answer

after the universe asked *why?* -
life has never once looked at you

and picked up a red pen.
I want you to know

your *one days*
turn into *at lasts*,

I want you to know
you're gonna make it.

To thirteen-year-old me (and all the other kids carrying worry around in their schoolbags) - *A further note*

You want to be the same
as everyone else.

You have no idea that everyone else
wants to be the same as everyone else.

You have no idea that maybe everyone else
wants to be like you.

Four billion beautiful things

In 2016, a Dove beauty study found only four percent of women around the world call themselves beautiful. If you often find yourself in the other ninety-six percent, this poem is for you.

Long before you were even born
Beautiful got down on one knee

and vowed to spend forever
on the third finger of your left hand -

I don't know why
you stopped wearing your ring.

Don't hide your worth
like your face is a self-portrait

and your valuables
are hidden behind it in a wall safe.

You are the kind of beautiful
that makes money

drop itself into slot machines
and pray to come out

with enough reinforcements to cover every down
payment on your up-turned mouth.

Every time your mouth says, *lift-off*
Helen of Troy turns in her gorgeous grave

her face may have launched
a thousand ships

but dear god
yours is Cape Canaveral,

every rocket-ship with stars in its eyes
started out on the launch pad of your lips.

Make-up artists take contour sticks
and write your name

across their clients' cheekbones -
this is how they light up a face.

Once upon a time,
the cleverest minds

believed light
had to be carried around inside something,

they called it *luminiferous aether*
until discoveries declared it did not exist -

you prove science wrong
every time you smile and take a step.

With each one of those steps, never forget
there is a place in Antarctica

known as the Kodak Gap -
it's so beautiful

it's impossible
to take a bad photo there.

I think the Kodak Gap
is wherever you are standing.

Luciferin is the property within fireflies
that makes them shine

your beautiful is the luciferin
of someone's down days.

Maybe you feel broken some days
but if beauty didn't come from broken things

we wouldn't have Cheddar Gorge
and you are the grandest canyon to appear

after the earth cracked open
a bottle and all the rock unzipped itself.

Your face is a picture,
the kind of mug

shot that feels like caffeine –
you keep us up at night.

Your beautiful is not skin
alone, goes so deep below the surface

submarines whisper your name
at slumber parties

but if you will still not call yourself beautiful,
instead call

deed poll,
tell them you're changing your name to Presto,

then when you look in the mirror you can say *hey, Presto*
and finally know you make magic.

Because the same study that found
only four percent of women call themselves beautiful

also found eighty percent see something beautiful
in all other women.

So, tomorrow when you look in the mirror
I hope instead you can make it a window

to every other woman in this world
that way you will see

four billion beautiful things
and every one of them

will be you.

To *regret*

Tomorrow, I plan to forget
you, but you are stubborn,
made from icicles,

all the while I'm in the house
you still cling
to the front porch.

Tomorrow I will buy a blowtorch
and watch you melt
into a memory I will neglect to collect,

you will simply evaporate.
One rainy day you will fall on my face
and I won't even recognise you.

My melanin

My melanin is Black history month
all year.

My melanin is a barista,
makes an espresso so full-bodied,
a flat white buys a butt implant.

When night falls, my melanin catches it
understands how to hold darkness in its hands
and make moonlight from lifelines.

If you choose to believe in miracles
you can make a magic wand of a matchstick,
my melanin is nature's greatest magic trick -
absorbs sunlight like Palmer's cocoa butter.

My melanin's spirit animal
is not always a panther,
sometimes it is a poem
by Maya Angelou.

My melanin knows if you could mix
LaBelle's *Lady Marmalade*
with Beyonce's *Lemonade*,
I would never put anything else in my mouth.

My melanin was told it was *the ace of spades*
but is too busy being the queen of hearts.

My melanin says *I matter*
and sometimes I have to sit
and relearn restraint,
teach my melanin why Diversity
caused 24,000 Ofcom complaints.

My melanin is a lion,
my country thinks itself a ringmaster
but this DNA remembers the whip
so, as the lion sleeps tonight, it dreams
of how to swallow micro-aggression and spit
out its bones.

The skin is the largest organ
of the body, just as an organ
is the largest instrument in a church
my melanin sits every day
singing prayers in the front pew.

You can't just pick this shade
off the shelf at B&Q,
my melanin took millennia,
is ten thousand generations
of lovemaking in the mix,
my melanin is Mother Nature
and Father Time's favourite kid.

My melanin is a geography GCSE,
God's tour de force
and the only certain way
to navigate stars at sea,

when it is told to go back
where it came from,
my melanin says,
*then show me the way
to the beginning.*

And at the end,
in a billion years,
when the sun spins the last slow song
on the solar sound system,
begins the breakdown of a supernova,

since melanin holds light
like Galileo's telescope held the moon,
the universe will suck
all the oxygen out of the room,

marvel how a star exploding
in the vastness of infinity -
just makes my melanin look good.

How *carefree* came to be

There was once a bird with thoughts
for wings and every time it flew, it knew,

never to overthink things -

or it would get tired
and fall out of the sky.

How to stop your spiralling head with your soaring heart

Stop
just stop it now

live
keep living

keep right on living
until your lifeline runs out of runway

so, you have no choice
but to try and fly

next time you notice joy
stop acting so shy

go right up to it and say *hi*
tell me everything about yourself

when self-talk sends you junk mail
click unsubscribe

live wide
make reckless your new career

take down every stop sign
on the road to your heart

try to break
every speed limit here

on the days getting out of bed
seems like war, remember Monaco

has an orchestra bigger than its army
and you can too

so many people love to hear your tune
smile enough so when the moon

forgets to shine it searches your face
on Google to remember how to light up a room

the book of you
is a work in progress

who cares if you tear
a few pages on the way

the library is open and someone out there
can't wait to read you today

stop worrying about that thing
and go dance in your pants in the kitchen

make Cinderella your Jesus
since *have courage and be kind*

makes more sense than anything you find
in the bible

tell anyone who will listen that your name is a verb
there is so much you can do

next time someone asks your opinion
speak it loud enough to drop every mic

and take a stand instead
put your whole soul on speakerphone

know whatever the time
you are not too late -

a man named Momofoku Ando
was almost fifty when he made history

inventing instant ramen noodles -
if he can change the world selling 3D doodles

you can do any damn thing

tell yourself time is a Belgian waffle
then you will never feel bad for eating your way through it

because one morning
you're going to wonder

what to have for breakfast, blissful
in the ignorance it will be your last one

so, stop
just stop it now

take life by its lapels
pull life close

look deep into life's eyes
like life just told you it loves you

get into a staring competition with life
and for once
don't you dare look away first.

How *healing* came to be

The cartographer learned how to be a clockmaker and took one step at a time. The minutes became miles. The miles became months. The months grew legs, and the years began to stand up on their own. But the cardiologist never left their chest. Many birthday cakes later, the cartographer became a cobbler and constructed themselves a new pair of shoes that could only ever walk in a different direction. But once in a while they walked too quickly, just to remember how it felt when their heart beat faster.

Home

I once read that fingerprints are formed from touching
our mother's wombs. Somewhere deep inside
my first home is the echo of my earliest cave painting.
My mother still has my first poem on the walls.

Where I live now the trains go to bed early
on weekends, like the town is terrified
if we stay out late, we won't come back.
And there are signs

on the beach that warn against the danger of disappearing
in the mud, but we still buy candy floss
and put sticks in our mouths. From a distance
a stick of rock and a stick of dynamite

don't look so different – it's hard to tell
if you hold sweetness or explosion in your hands
and isn't that another way to say
what does it feel like to be alive?

Where I live now there is a man in a van
who roams the streets every Saturday
calling out for our spare metals
and I wonder if people still have any old iron, lying

around waiting for a new home.
Then I remember metals are already recycled,
formed from dying stars - there isn't much difference
between an ironmonger and an astronaut.

Isn't this how we all started out -
we've been together since the Big Bang banged big
and spilled theories all over the carpet of the cosmos,
our elements bonded, held hands

and waited for the dust to settle.
We all come from the same stars, same town
what is this life but the last train home
when we wish they ran a little later,

we're all just getting right back where we started.
I live here now, yesterday I lived there,
one day my mother left her mark
on my fingertips, someday I'll settle

on your eyelashes
and in a blink, you'll miss me
but I'll be around again soon.
I'll see you when you get home.

To-do list for a life
After Andrea Gibson

To say sorry
only for something I did,
never for something I am.

To accept some people
won't like me and that's okay -
as long as I am not one of them.

To stand against storms
like the Lighthouse on Legs,
be guided not by my head
but the lightbulbs in my chest.

To grow like the first sweet daffodil
that ever forced itself through the frost
on the side of the road, to show,
good things can come from being on the verge.

To sing through the sad times,
as though a gospel choir got stuck in my throat
and embrace every shaky note,
like it is a love letter written in a nervous hand.

To understand
this body is the best birthday present I ever got, to not
try to exchange it for store credit.

To refuse to spend
time trying to be someone else,

there's nobody better to be than myself –
even Michelangelo only became successful
after he failed at art fraud.

To pay attention in the scary moments,
never hide behind the fingers of my own life.

To write like my fingers
are a Dictaphone for delight.

To find as much joy in the Wednesdays
as the weekends.

To adore winter the same way I worship spring –
isn't it all just puddles and piles of leaves,
so, what is winter anyway, but nature whispering,
I dare you to jump in.

To never make the first question I ask a stranger,
so, what do you do for a living? But only,
shiny new friend, what do you do to feel alive?

To live like kindness is a skydive
and I can't stop throwing myself out of planes.

To remind myself in the moments I'm at the top,
pride is a spiral staircase. To know my ego
is a tantrum in need of a naughty step.

To recognise some days now
I am a lonely car on the carriageway
and grief is a persistent hitchhiker.
When sadness sticks out its thumb,
I will pull over and invite it in,

say, *let's play all the old songs -*
but I can only take you so far down the road.

To disbelieve the bedtime stories
my self-talk reads,
my inner saboteur is nothing
but an audiobook
and I just cancelled my Audible subscription.

To stop living like a limbo stick
and see my self-esteem as an unshakeable
pole vault bar, to stay up high
no matter who comes to try
and get one over on me.

To be the big brave
when I feel the small broken,
to be the small broken a little less this year.

To keep faith like Henry Lewis, the oldest person
on the 2022 New Years Honours list -
if a 102-year-old magician can live through the last century
and still believe in magic, anything is possible.

To go gentle with myself
without asking others to do it first.
To be the first nail to tell the hammer
thanks, but I'll make my own way in.

To let go of my insecurities,
the way the clouds let go of themselves.

To laugh at myself, sure
every time I fall down

the universe is doing stand up
comedy, every embarrassment is my soul
saying *your cheeks needed warming anyway.*

To acknowledge I am both light and dark
as a developing photograph,
some days my head is covered in halos
other's horns – but hell,
there's grace and angels.

To do the damn thing
like I am the last descendent of every grandfather
clock and time is wearing out its running shoes.

To tell everyone I love
I'll always be your parachute
or your cowboy. Pull my cord
and I'll tell you to reach for the sky
or I'll catch you in it. Either way, my heartstrings
are forever waiting for your fingers.

To love every moment
of this gorgeous, clusterfuck chaos theory of a life,
even when those theories become reality.

And then to remember anyway,
all this reality is just the time between trains.
To simply be thankful
we were at the same station today.

The end

I hope life
is a stubborn houseguest
that never knows when to leave,
blissful and unaware
of overstaying its welcome.

I hope life
sticks around so long, fate
gets off the sofa,
stretches its arms
to the top of the world
and yawns, *well, it's getting late...*

ACKNOWLEDGEMENTS

I heard the secret to happiness 'is to surround yourself with people who make your heart smile.'
Thank you, thank you, thank you to the following folks who truly get my heart grinning:

Chris Halliday and Kirsty Jones, for being the fearless and fabulous beta-readers of this book. And to Kat Lyons and Jemima Hughes, for writing such beautiful words about it.

Simon Stone, fantastic photographer (and Jedi legend) for gifting me his gorgeous photograph for the cover.

Stuart Bartholomew and Verve Poetry Press for providing a wonderful wall to display my art - I'm so grateful to be part of your gallery.

The amazing and supportive poetry and creative community in Bristol, Weston-Super-Mare and beyond - particularly the folks at Raise the Bar, Satellite of Love, St. George's, Rhyme against the Tide and Oooh Beehive, who have given me so many fantastic opportunities to share and showcase my writing.

My family and friends, there are around 170,000 words currently in use in the English language - and I still can't find enough ways to say how much I love you all.

My mum - thanks for all those Ladybird books, back when we didn't have much, we always had words. Thanks for every one of them. I love you so many millions.

Shakira, my partner in life and crime and wondering what to watch, I love you the very much mostest. This book would not have existed without you ... and very nearly didn't - thank you for kicking me up the bum with the boots in your mouth!

My best friend. I love you and I miss you.

And finally, yourself, dear reader - I was looking everywhere for you, and you were right here this whole time. I can't wait until our paths link arms again.

ALSO AVAILABLE FROM VERVEPOETRYPRESS.COM

Where Else:
An International Hong Kong Poetry Anthology

With an introduction from the editors

Featuring both established and emerging Hong Kong poets across generations and continents, this unique anthology offers a glimpse into an exciting, diverse range of voices that make up the diasporic imagination of the contemporary Hong Kong poetry community. Adopting a diasporic approach, the anthology encompasses both native Hong Kong writers as well as expatriate and mixed-race voices who were born or have lived in the city.

Includes poems from Sarah Howe, Kit Fan, Jennifer Wong, Mary Jean Chan, Eric Yip, Tim Tim Cheng, Sean Wai Keung and many more.

Available in paperback:
ISBN: 978 1 917913 36 4
252 pages • 216 x 138 • 106 poems
£14.99

And on eBook:
ISBN: 978 1 913917 79 1
£9.99

ALSO AVAILABLE FROM VERVEPOETRYPRESS.COM

Into The Ordinary
Jemima Hughes

Incredible second collection from Birmingham based poetry bomb Jemima!

This is not out of the ordinary. This is commonplace.

Following on from her storming, debut poetry collection *Unorthodox*, Jemima Hughes sits with you in the aftermath to discuss how to rebuild. Jemima's story is one of sexual violence trauma and mental health difficulties but, ultimately, it is a story of hope.

'Jemima has a way of transporting you through darkness and into light through her words and her performance. When she writes she captures a reality that so many of us find ourselves in, and when she performes she takes us all there.' - Casey Bailey

Available in paperback:
ISBN: 978 1 912565 40 1
136 pages • 216 x 168 • 42 poems
£10.99

ABOUT VERVE POETRY PRESS

Verve Poetry Press is an award-winning press that focused initially on meeting a local need in Birmingham - a need for the vibrant poetry scene here in Brum to find a way to present itself to the poetry world via publication. Co-founded by Stuart Bartholomew and Amerah Saleh, it now publishes poets from all corners of the UK - poets that speak to the city's varied and energetic qualities and will contribute to its many poetic stories.

Added to this is a colourful pamphlet series, many featuring poets who have performed at our sister festival - and a poetry show series which captures the magic of longer poetry performance pieces by festival alumni such as Polarbear, Matt Abbott and Imogen Stirling.

The press has been voted Most Innovative Publisher at the Saboteur Awards, and has won the Publisher's Award for Poetry Pamphlets at the Michael Marks Awards.

Like the festival, we strive to think about poetry in inclusive ways and embrace the multiplicity of approaches towards this glorious art.

www.vervepoetrypress.com
@VervePoetryPres
mail@vervepoetrypress.com